Original title:
Frost-Kissed Woods

Copyright © 2024 Swan Charm
All rights reserved.

Author: Olivia Orav
ISBN HARDBACK: 978-9916-79-432-6
ISBN PAPERBACK: 978-9916-79-433-3
ISBN EBOOK: 978-9916-79-434-0

Draped in Silver

A blanket of frost lies soft and still,
Moonlight drapes the world in silvery chill.
Whispers of night dance on the breeze,
In the quiet glow, hearts find their ease.

Trees stand tall with branches bare,
Each one a sentinel of the cold air.
Stars twinkle gently in the deep sky,
As shadows shift and old dreams sigh.

Shimmering Light

Morning breaks with a golden glow,
Soft beams of warmth in which to grow.
Radiant colors paint the sky bright,
Transforming the world with shimmering light.

Petals awake to kiss the dawn,
Nature's symphony gently drawn.
Each sunbeam dances on dewy lace,
In this vibrant, sacred space.

The Hidden Path Beneath a Shroud of White

A path unfolds in blankets of snow,
Mysteries lie where only brave go.
Footsteps echo in the quiet air,
Whispers of magic beckon with flare.

Beneath the surface, secrets await,
Each turn and curve a twist of fate.
Journey onward through frost and ice,
Embrace the unknown, it feels so nice.

Celestial Patterns in Nature's Quilt

Stars stitched together in night's embrace,
Patterns of beauty in endless space.
Leaves shimmer softly, reflecting the light,
Nature's quilt glows under moon's sight.

Every thread woven with stories untold,
In colors of twilight, both vibrant and bold.
From mountains to rivers, the designs expand,
A tapestry woven by time's gentle hand.

Elysium in Icicles and Pine

In winter's grasp, where silence reigns,
Icicles hang like nature's chains.
Pine trees whisper secrets to the breeze,
A tranquil sanctuary among frozen trees.

Sunlight filters through the crystal clear,
A serene place to linger near.
In the heart of cold, warmth intertwines,
Elysium dwells in the mountains of pines.

Glistening Prayers on a Cold Night

The moonlight spills on frozen ground,
Whispers of hopes that softly sound.
Stars twinkle bright, like jewels untold,
Each one a wish, a prayer to hold.

Chilled winds carry tales from afar,
Of dreams ignited by a single star.
The night wraps tight with its velvet embrace,
Cradling heartbeats, a serene space.

Shadows dance where the branches sway,
Every breath of frost leads the way.
In silence, I find my spirit flow,
A warmth igniting, despite the snow.

Embers of hope in a blanket of cold,
Fires of faith, endlessly bold.
We gather together, in whispers of light,
Holding glistening prayers through the night.

Morning will come with a soft, tender glow,
Yet till then, in the stillness, we'll grow.
Each frozen moment, a promise, a sight,
Glistening prayers on this cold, starry night.

Frosted Luminescence in the Secret Wood

In hidden glades where shadows play,
The trees wear frost like a silvery ray.
Crystals glisten on the boughs so tall,
Whispering secrets, nature's call.

Footsteps muffled on a snowy trail,
Guided by moonlight, the softest veil.
Each breath I take, a cloud softly shared,
The magic of winter, beautifully bared.

A sparkling stream flows, a gentle sound,
Reflecting stars that dance all around.
In this secret wood, time stands still,
Heartbeats echo with each tranquil thrill.

The world fades away, a hushed reprise,
Wrapped in the splendor of frosted skies.
Every moment, a treasure bestowed,
Illuminated softly in the secret wood.

Embraced by the quiet of snowy night,
Glistening visions, a breathtaking sight.
Together with shadows, I'll linger and stay,
In frosted luminescence, forever I'll play.

Shivering Leaves in the Quiet Dawn

In the hush of morning light,
Leaves shiver, kissed by dew,
Whispers dance on gentle air,
Nature's secret, old and new.

Branches bend, in soft embrace,
A world awakes, calm and slow,
Sunrise paints with golden grace,
The silent beauty on show.

Birds begin their shy refrain,
Songs of joy fill the still,
As shadows stretch across the lane,
And hearts embrace the chill.

With each breath, the earth ignites,
Flickers of light chase away,
The lingering hold of night,
Welcoming the breaking day.

In these moments, peace ascends,
Time stands still within its fold,
Nature breathes, as life extends,
Shivering leaves, a tale untold.

Icy Breath of Woodland Spirits

In the woods where shadows loom,
Breath of frost, a silent song,
Whispers weave through ancient gloom,
Dancing spirits, soft and strong.

Branches wear their crystal crowns,
Glistening with winter's touch,
Nature dons her sparkling gowns,
Each heartbeat whispers, 'Feel the hush.'

Frozen streams like mirrors shine,
Reflecting dreams of twinkling stars,
In this realm, the world aligns,
Silence wrapped in silver bars.

Mossy stones, a sacred ground,
Echoes of the night's embrace,
In this beauty, peace is found,
Woodland spirits weave their grace.

Faintest sighs of life persist,
Underneath the icy sweep,
Within the cold, a warm tryst,
Awakens all that lies asleep.

Enchanted Shadows in December's Hold

Beneath the sky, a solemn grey,
Shadows stretch on ancient stone,
In December's gentle sway,
The world feels both lost and known.

Frosted boughs, a silent choir,
Singing softly through the night,
In their stillness, dreams inspire,
Guiding souls with hidden light.

Mist entwines with winter's breath,
A warmth that cloaks the dreary chill,
Life and death entwined in depth,
Each heartbeat holds the magic still.

Glistening paths that twist and wound,
In the woodland's secret fold,
Whispers of the lost, profound,
As stories of the past are told.

In the heart of winter's spell,
Hope arises, pure and bright,
Amidst the chill, we know so well,
Love endures through darkest night.

Glimmering Echoes of the Frosted Night

In the stillness of the night,
Frosty flakes begin to glide,
Moonbeams cast a silver light,
As the stars in silence bide.

Whispers of the icy breeze,
Carry tales through woods and glen,
Nature breathes in soft decrees,
Echoes linger, time and again.

Glistening paths of white and blue,
Lead the wanderer anew,
Underneath a sky so true,
Magic thickens in the dew.

Frosted whispers, soft and clear,
Speak of secrets held so tight,
In their embrace, we draw near,
Finding solace in the night.

With dawn awaiting just in sight,
The world prepares for day's delight,
Yet in the dark, dreams take flight,
In glimmering echoes of the night.

Shards of Glass Amidst the Twisting Roots

In the forest where shadows creep,
Shards of glass in silence weep.
Twisting roots like fingers grasp,
Whispers of time in their clasp.

Reflections dance on fallen leaves,
As nature sighs, the heart believes.
Each fragment tells a story lost,
In the embrace of beauty's cost.

Colorful shards, a fleeting light,
Dancing softly, a splendid sight.
Echoes linger, the past entwined,
Within the roots, a gold mine blind.

Underneath the ancient trees,
The glass sings soft on gentle breeze.
Secrets hide where eyes can't see,
Among the roots, forever free.

Shattered dreams in earth confined,
Yet, in their chaos, truths aligned.
Beauty found in broken pieces,
Life's mosaic, as time ceases.

Serenades of Stillness in Nature's Arms

In amber light, the day unfolds,
A serenade of whispers told.
Nature cradles time and space,
In her arms, we find our place.

Softly swaying, branches sway,
Caressing thoughts that drift away.
Every moment, a gentle pause,
Embraced by life's tender cause.

Silence echoes through the glade,
In every brook, the calm cascades.
The rustling leaves, a soothing song,
In nature's arms, we all belong.

Birds on wing, a fleeting trace,
In this stillness, we find grace.
The world outside may pulse and race,
Yet here, we bask in warm embrace.

Stars arise as daylight dims,
Nature whets our spirit's whims.
In her bosom, peace is found,
In stillness, love knows no bound.

The Chill of Serenity in the Twilight Wood

Twilight falls on silent glades,
The chill of night, a soft cascade.
Whispers of dusk weave through the trees,
In their grasp, a gentle breeze.

Serene shadows stretch and yawn,
As daylight fades and night is born.
The wood speaks secrets, rich and deep,
In twilight's grasp, the world sleeps.

Each step muffled on the ground,
In this calm, no harshness found.
Moonlight weaves through branches bare,
In the stillness, we find care.

Breath of frost upon the air,
A moment held, a tranquil stare.
The chill wraps round like a warm embrace,
In twilight's grip, we find our place.

Here, serenity takes its hold,
In nature's arms, stories unfold.
Under stars, our spirits free,
In the chill, we find harmony.

Starlit Dreams on the Frosted Path

Underneath a blanket bright,
Starlit dreams find their flight.
Frosted steps on crispest ground,
In the stillness, magic found.

Every twinkle calls our name,
A universe, not just a game.
Each breath a cloud, soft and white,
As we walk through the velvet night.

Whispers carried on the air,
Boundless wonders everywhere.
The frosted path, a canvas wide,
Painted dreams where hopes abide.

Celestial fire in the sky,
Bids us dance, invites our sigh.
As starlight drapes the world in grace,
Every heartbeat, a sacred space.

With every step, we uncover more,
The essence of dreams, an open door.
On the frosted trail, we roam,
In starlit realms, we find our home.

Beneath a Blanket of Silvered Dust

Snowflakes dance in fragile flight,
Whispers softly greet the night.
A blanket drapes the world in white,
Dreams awaken in gentle light.

Silvery shadows softly gleam,
Underneath the moon's pale beam.
Quiet secrets in the frost,
In winter's hold, we find what's lost.

Branches bowed with heavy grace,
Nature's calm, a warm embrace.
In the silence, hearts align,
Beneath the stars, your hand in mine.

Footsteps crunch on powdered ground,
Echoes of the peace we've found.
Each moment wrapped in crystal hue,
Together here, just me and you.

As dawn breaks, a canvas bright,
The world awakens, pure delight.
With each breath, the chill subsides,
Beneath this dust, our love abides.

The Winter's Breath upon the Pines

A silver sigh through branches weaves,
A tranquil hush that nature leaves.
Amongst the pines, the whispers play,
As winter's breath brings forth the day.

Frosted needles catch the light,
Glittering gems in morning bright.
With each gust, a tale unfolds,
Stories of warmth that winter holds.

Beneath the boughs, the world turns slow,
In every flake, a spark, a glow.
The forest breathes in chilly air,
And dreams of spring begin to stir.

A tapestry of white and green,
Nature's wonder, pure and keen.
In the quiet, peace we find,
A bond that time cannot unwind.

As evening falls with velvet skies,
The stars emerge, a sweet surprise.
Each breath, a promise stitched in time,
A timeless dance, both yours and mine.

Frigid Serenade in a Silent Grove

In the grove, the silence reigns,
Frigid whispers chill the veins.
A serenade of icy breath,
Awakens dreams, a dance with death.

Moonlit shadows weave and flow,
Tracing paths where time moves slow.
Crystalline beauty cloaks the trees,
In this winter's hush, we freeze.

Echoes linger in the air,
Songs of ages, hearts laid bare.
Nature's lullaby, soft and light,
Guides us through the velvet night.

Each branch adorned with frozen tears,
A symphony that calms our fears.
With every sigh, a promise grows,
In the cold, our love still glows.

As dawn approaches, shadows fade,
Yet memories of warmth are laid.
In this silent grove, we stand,
Frigid serenade, hand in hand.

Glacial Veil on Elder Pathways

Ancient trees in quiet stand,
Bearing witness, timeless, grand.
A glacial veil wraps every lane,
Muffled footsteps, soft as rain.

Each pathway whispers tales of old,
Secrets buried, stories told.
Underneath the icy sheen,
Lies a world where dreams convene.

The frosty air, a crisp embrace,
In this stillness, find our place.
With every breath, the past ignites,
Guiding love through winter nights.

In corners where the shadows play,
Our hearts, a bright and fierce display.
As stars appear and darkness swells,
We're wrapped in magic, where love dwells.

Though time may pass with winter's chill,
This glacial veil can't break our will.
Through elder pathways, side by side,
In snowy dreams, forever glide.

Whispers of Winter's Breath

Chill winds murmur through the trees,
While snowflakes fall like whispered dreams.
The world in silence, soft and pale,
Wrapped in winter's cozy veil.

Frosted branches, crystals gleam,
A tranquil hush, a winter's theme.
Footsteps crunch on icy ground,
In this stillness, peace is found.

Moonlight dances on the snow,
Casting shadows, soft and low.
A breath of cold, a fleeting sigh,
As night embraces, stars drift by.

Breath of winter, crisp and bright,
Holds the magic of the night.
Every flake, a story told,
In the quiet, brave and bold.

Nature sleeps in soft repose,
Under blankets white it goes.
With dawn, a new day to unfold,
Whispers of winter, quiet and gold.

Silver Shadows Beneath the Boughs

In the twilight, shadows play,
Beneath the trees, where whispers sway.
Silver leaves in softest light,
Guide the way through coming night.

Branches arch like gentle arms,
Holding secrets, nature's charms.
Underneath, the earth lies still,
Waiting for the moon's goodwill.

Softly glows the silver mist,
In the silence, winds persist.
Each shadow dances, light and dark,
A tranquil world, a quiet spark.

Footsteps linger, heartbeats swell,
In the woods where stories dwell.
Every rustle, sweet as song,
Beneath the boughs where we belong.

As night unveils its secret hue,
Silver shadows call to you.
Join the dance, embrace the night,
In the stillness, find delight.

Glimmers of Ice on Aged Bark

Ancient trees stand wise and tall,
Nature's tales they recall.
Glimmers of ice on weathered skin,
Reflect the stories held within.

Each crack and crevice, time embraced,
In every layer, a life traced.
Shimmering frost, a delicate lace,
Adorns the bark with gentle grace.

Sunlight dances, bright and keen,
Through branches clad in winter's sheen.
Nature's art, a fleeting sight,
In the day, so fresh and bright.

As shadows lengthen, colors fade,
Whispers of twilight serenade.
The forest breathes a calming sigh,
As night descends, the stars reply.

In the stillness, peace we find,
A connection to the ancient kind.
Glimmers of ice, forever bark,
Witness to life in beauty stark.

A Dance of Crystal Petals

In gardens dressed in winter's lace,
Crystal petals share their grace.
Softly gliding, winds entwine,
Nature's breath, a pure design.

Above, the sky, a canvas gray,
Below, the frost in bright display.
Each petal glimmers, pure and fine,
A fleeting dance, a gift divine.

Branches bow with weight of dew,
As sunshine breaks the clouds in blue.
Here in silence, joy unfolds,
In each petal, a memory holds.

The world a stage, so calm, so clear,
Where every whisper speaks sincere.
A dance of beauty softly sung,
In every heart, forever young.

As twilight waltzes into night,
Petals shimmer in fading light.
Nature's dance, a timeless quest,
In crystal beauty, we find rest.

The Icy Caress of Nature's Hand

Frost kisses the earth so white,
Trees sparkle in the pale moonlight.
A hush falls softly through the night,
Nature sleeps, all wrapped up tight.

Crystals gleam on every bough,
Whispers of winter, quiet vow.
A chill that dances on the brow,
In this stillness, we wonder how.

Paths of silver stretch so far,
Guided by a single star.
With every step, the heart will spar,
In the glow of the winter spar.

A breath of cold, so sweetly shared,
In this realm, we feel unpaired.
Each moment lingers, deeply cared,
In the beauty that is bared.

Hold on tight, the magic sways,
In the crispness of winter's gaze.
Time stands still, the world obeys,
In the icy hand, our hearts amaze.

Moonlit Trails in Enchanted Thickets

Through thickets dense, the moonlight streams,
Casting shadows, weaving dreams.
A path where nature softly gleams,
In the silence, magic seems.

Whispers travel on the breeze,
Rustling leaves among the trees.
Each step stirs the night with ease,
A symphony of twinkling keys.

Flickers dance on winding trails,
Guided by the nightingale's wails.
Every twist of fate unveils,
The secrets in the moonlit gales.

Crickets chirp their lullabies,
As the night unfolds and sighs.
Underneath the velvet skies,
We wander where the magic lies.

In this thicket, we become,
Part of nature's silent hum.
In the moon's embrace, we succumb,
To the joy that always comes.

Secrets Hidden Under a Blanket of Frost

Beneath the frost, the world holds tight,
Stories buried, out of sight.
A whispered truth in the pale twilight,
A realm where stillness meets delight.

Frosty petals, delicate lace,
Nature's art in a frozen space.
In every nook, we find a trace,
Of secrets held in winter's embrace.

Frozen whispers call the brave,
To seek the tales that winter gave.
In the quiet, heartbeats wave,
Lost in dreams, we gently crave.

Underneath, the life awaits,
In cycles spun by time's own fates.
With each dawn, the old abates,
Revealing wonders behind the gates.

So tread softly, dear explorer,
Through the realms of icy horror.
The frost conceals the past's decor,
In its grasp, lies evermore.

The Lullaby of Shivering Branches

Underneath the pale moon's glow,
Branches sway in a soft woe.
Each rustle sings of tales below,
The lullaby of trees in snow.

As gentle winds begin to play,
Nature weaves its night ballet.
In the dark, the shadows sway,
A nursery rhyme in soft array.

Crickets hum their evening tune,
As branches tremble, kissed by moon.
In the stillness, hearts attune,
To the night's embrace, a sweet boon.

With every shiver, stories swell,
Of ancient trees that weave their spell.
In the cold, there's warmth to dwell,
The whispers of the night compel.

So when the frosty air does bite,
Find solace in the quiet night.
The lullaby of branches bright,
Will cradle you in purest light.

The Enfolded Magic of a Winter's Night

Stars glitter like diamonds bright,
Under the cloak of soft moonlight.
Whispers of snowflakes grace the air,
Woven tales of dreams laid bare.

Silent woods in slumber deep,
Crystals frozen, secrets keep.
A fire's glow, a warm embrace,
In winter's heart, a sweet, soft place.

Frosted branches, nature's art,
Glistening jewels close to the heart.
Breath hangs heavy, a ghostly mist,
In the magic, we simply exist.

Echoes of laughter, children play,
In a world where night swallows day.
Dreams unfold like petals pure,
In winter's magic, we find our cure.

Hold on tight, these moments bright,
In the magic of a winter's night.

Breaths of Clarity on Frosted Vistas

The dawn awakens, crisp and clear,
Frosted breath in the chilly sphere.
Footprints crunch on the glistening ground,
Whispers of nature, a gentle sound.

Trees stand wrapped in winter's lace,
A silent beauty, a serene space.
Hues of blue and silver gleam,
In this world, we weave our dream.

Each step forward, clarity reigns,
In the stillness, peace remains.
Mountains rise with majesty high,
Beneath the vast, unyielding sky.

Birds take flight, a graceful dance,
In frosted vistas, we find our chance.
To breathe in life, to cherish the day,
In nature's arms, we yearn to stay.

Views like paintings, rich and bright,
Breaths of clarity, pure delight.

Reflections on a Wintery Stream

A stream flows softly, a silver thread,
Reflecting dreams where wishes are spread.
Icicles dangle, sharp as a sigh,
Winter's whispers beneath the sky.

Rippling waters dance with glee,
Carving paths through winter's spree.
Shimmering surfaces, glassy and bright,
Hold secrets of day and whispers of night.

The air feels thick with stories unsaid,
In every ripple, the past is fed.
Moments captured in a fleeting glance,
Like footprints fading in a trance.

Hope floats lightly on winter's breath,
As nature weaves the fabric of death.
Each drop a memory, floating downstream,
Lost in the currents, like a dream.

Reflections shimmer, alive and profound,
In the wintery stream, we are found.

The Sibilant Touch of Icy Dreams

In the hush of night, dreams take flight,
The sibilant touch of icy light.
Shadows dance on a silent floor,
As magic lingers, forevermore.

Glistening whispers grace the air,
With every breath, the night we share.
Secrets held in the frozen dew,
In the stillness, the earth renews.

Gentle sighs of winter's breath,
In the calm, we confront our death.
Embrace the chill, the cool caress,
In icy dreams, we find our rest.

Frosted mirrors of a tranquil soul,
In winter's hold, we become whole.
An ethereal dance where shadows sway,
In the icy breath, we softly play.

The world transformed, a crystal gleam,
In the sibilant touch of icy dreams.

Resonance of Winter in the Ancient Grove

The ancient trees stand tall and bare,
Whispers of frost fill the brisk air.
Silent echoes of memories past,
Embracing winter, holding fast.

Snowflakes dance in a gentle sway,
Branches adorned in white display.
Each creak of bark sings a tune,
In the hush of a pale afternoon.

Frozen streams, with quiet flow,
Reflecting secrets of days aglow.
Nature's breath in chilly sighs,
Carving paths where the snowbird flies.

Footprints linger, stories told,
Where shadows mingle with the cold.
In the grove, time moves so slow,
As winter weaves its timeless show.

Beneath the moon's soft silver light,
Glimmers weave through the heart of night.
The ancient grove in frosty shrouds,
Awakens dreams amidst the clouds.

Memories Like Snowflakes in the Breeze

Fleeting moments like snowflakes fall,
Whispers of laughter, a distant call.
Each flake unique, a story spun,
Drifting softly, one by one.

Memory glimmers, bright and clear,
Lost in the shadows, drawing near.
A soft chill carries the past's embrace,
Like winter's touch in a quiet space.

Eyes closed tight, I breathe the air,
Scent of nostalgia, floating fair.
Echoes of joy amidst the chill,
Filling the silence, time stands still.

A gentle wind, it stirs the day,
Chasing soft thoughts that drift away.
With every breath, the past arrives,
In the dance of snow, memory thrives.

Through the cold, I find my way,
In the warmth of what used to stay.
Like snowflakes swaying, free and true,
Each memory beckons, calling you.

Lightfooted Whispers Upon the Snow

Footsteps gentle upon the white,
Whispers trace paths in the night.
Soft as feathers, they glide and weave,
Secrets held in the chill of eve.

Snow-draped branches dream and sigh,
Under the vast and starry sky.
Children's laughter through frosty air,
Dancing lightly without a care.

Echoes of joy in the cold they sing,
Each note a tender, fleeting wing.
Frost-laden air, crisp and sweet,
In this moment, we feel complete.

Twilight wraps the world in grace,
Friendly shadows start to chase.
Lightfooted whispers glide like ghosts,
In winter's arms, warmth we toast.

The night holds secrets, pure and mild,
In snowflakes, winter's dreams reside.
Together we walk, a shared delight,
As whispers linger in the night.

The Enigmatic Embrace of the Cold

In the stillness, a chill draws near,
The world wrapped close, quiet and clear.
Frosted windows frame the view,
Each breath visible, sharp and new.

A lonesome wind begins to howl,
Its song a mysterious, haunting growl.
The trees stand guard, ancient and wise,
Under a cloak of silvered skies.

Each flake that falls seems to tell,
Secrets held within winter's spell.
The ground adorned in crystal lace,
Nature's art, a serene embrace.

As daylight fades, the shadows creep,
In the cold, the earth falls deep.
Whispers echo through the night,
Lost in the dark, out of sight.

The silent world in frozen thrall,
Each heartbeat echoes, soft and small.
Delicate moments wrapped in gold,
Caught in the enigmatic cold.

Nature's Still Heart amidst the Icicles

The stillness hangs in icy air,
Nature's breath a whispered prayer.
Icicles glisten like crystal tears,
Her heart beats softly through the years.

Branches cradle a frozen hue,
Snowflakes dance, a fleeting view.
Beneath the frost, life holds her dreams,
In quiet moments, peace redeems.

The sun peeks shyly, shy and bright,
Illuminating the serene night.
Nature sleeps in her winter dress,
A tranquil heart, boundless finesse.

Still lakes mirror the starry skies,
While echoes of the forest sighs.
In silence, wonder starts to spark,
Awakening life within the dark.

Ceaseless Whispers in the Winter Night

The moonlight drapes the world in white,
Whispers carry through the night.
Trees stand tall like ancient guards,
Their shadows etched in frozen yards.

A gentle breeze begins to weave,
Tales of warmth and dreams to leave.
Softly calling, the night birds sing,
Through the silence, their voices ring.

Footsteps crunch on paths of snow,
In secret glades where wild things grow.
A world transformed, a silent sight,
In ceaseless whispers, hearts take flight.

Stars twinkle in the velvet deep,
While the forest wraps in quiet sleep.
Nature's voice, both calm and wise,
In winter's arms, the spirit flies.

Frosted Vision in the Forest's Eyes

Frosted visions shimmer clear,
In the forest's eyes, we peer.
Every branch like delicate lace,
Captures beauty in its space.

Snowflakes twirl with graceful art,
Painting canvases from the start.
Icicles hang like thin-tongued swords,
Guardians of the earth's frail chords.

The wind whispers secrets old,
Tales of warmth in winter's cold.
Underneath the snow, life stirs,
A hidden world that gently purrs.

The silence sings in haunting notes,
Every creature, the forest gloats.
In frosted beauty, peace will rise,
Held in the forest's tranquil eyes.

Secrets Cradled in the Icebound Leaves

Secrets nestled in the freeze,
Cradled gently by the trees.
Leaves once lush now shimmer bright,
Transforming day into a night.

Silent stories in the frost,
Tell of moments that were lost.
In the stillness, time stands still,
Nature's heart, a rhythmic thrill.

Beneath the ice, the murmurs play,
Whispers of a warmer day.
The shivering branches bow their heads,
As snowflakes pillow sleepy beds.

Nature's canvas, pale and white,
Invites the stars to come alight.
Hidden truths, a soft embrace,
In icebound leaves, we find our place.

Echoes in the Chilled Canopy

In whispers soft, the branches sway,
Echoes dance where shadows play.
Frozen breath in twilight's gleam,
Nature hums a crystal dream.

A hush descends upon the leaves,
As dusk wraps all in silver weaves.
Footfalls muffled, silence calls,
Beneath the boughs, the stillness sprawls.

Frigid air, a gentle bite,
Guides the heart through fading light.
Each sound is rare, a fleeting note,
In this realm where dreams emote.

Branches cling to frozen skies,
Painting tales as time defies.
Echoes linger, soft and high,
Beneath the watchful, starry eye.

In chilled embrace, the world awaits,
A symphony of quiet fates.
While shadows blend in moonlit glow,
The whispers weave the tales we know.

The Whispering Silence of Snowbound Pines

The pines stand tall, a solemn choir,
Whispers drift through frost and fire.
Snowflakes fall, a soft adrift,
Nature's grace, a gentle gift.

Each branch adorned in winter's lace,
A quiet cloak, a peaceful space.
Beneath the snow, the earth breathes still,
Hidden tales that time will fill.

Resounding hush, a tranquil peace,
In this moment, all fears cease.
Hearts entwined with nature's sigh,
As dreams unfold beneath the sky.

In every drift, a story spun,
Of battles lost and victories won.
With every flake, a memory steals,
Carried forth on winter's wheels.

Among the trees, the silence reigns,
Scribbling thoughts on icy lanes.
The world holds breath in snowy grips,
As pines converse in whispered scripts.

Twilight's Embrace in the Frozen Grove

Twilight drapes in hues of blue,
Cloaking trees in evening's dew.
Frosted veins on ancient bark,
Breathe out warmth within the dark.

Glimmers dance on icy streams,
Reflecting all our fleeting dreams.
The frozen air, a crisp embrace,
Nestles softly in this place.

Branches touch as shadows blend,
Whispers fade as night descends.
In the stillness, secrets grow,
Bathed in twilight's soft, warm glow.

The grove enchants with muted light,
Turning echoes from day to night.
In this world, the heart does roam,
Finding solace, feeling home.

Stars awaken in the hush,
As the night wraps all in blush.
Together in this frozen cove,
Embrace the magic of the grove.

Beneath a Veil of Glimmering White

Beneath the veil, the world is hushed,
Covered in white, no need to rush.
Every flake, a whispered prayer,
Designed with love, floating in air.

Winter's quilt, a soft caress,
Enfolding all with quiet bless.
In every turn, a secret lies,
And in the silence, wisdom flies.

Crispness lingers in the breeze,
Awakening distant memories.
Footprints left in gentle grace,
Mark our path through this still space.

The trees, a gallery of dreams,
With diamond dust that subtly beams.
Every breath in frosty air,
Spins a story, unaware.

So here we stand, side by side,
In the glow of winter's tide.
Beneath this veil, we find our light,
In glimmering white and starry night.

Echoes of Dusk in the Quiet Forest

The trees stand tall, their shadows weave,
Whispers of twilight, as day begins to leave.
Soft colors blend in the waning light,
Nature's embrace wraps the coming night.

A distant call of a lone bird's song,
Echoing through branches, where shadows belong.
The forest breathes in a calming sigh,
While stars peek shyly from the vast, dark sky.

Mist curls gently, dancing on the ground,
Secrets of dusk in silence abound.
Soft rustlings hint at life close by,
As night descends with a watchful eye.

Glimmers of moonlight break through the trees,
Crickets begin their soft melodies.
The forest hums with a tranquil tune,
Awakening dreams that linger till noon.

Wrapped in peace, the world fades away,
As echoes of dusk kiss the end of day.
In this quiet place, where magic thrives,
The heart beats softly, where wonder lives.

Shadows of Blue in the Frosted Glade

Beneath the branches, a hush falls deep,
Shadows of blue in a world that sleeps.
Frost bites gently at the edges of leaves,
Whispers of winter that one hardly believes.

Glittering crystals hang in the air,
Subtle and stunning, a beautiful glare.
Each breath a cloud that rises and fades,
Carving soft paths in the frosted glades.

A gentle wind plays on the icy ground,
Filling the silence with a soothing sound.
The beauty of cold, so pure and bright,
Paints the landscape in silver light.

Footsteps crunch on the blanket of frost,
Tracing the beauty of moments long lost.
In shadows of blue, dreams softly collide,
Whispers of winter, nature's sweet guide.

Here time stands still, in a world so wide,
Finding the warmth that the cold cannot hide.
Eyes gaze in wonder, hearts gently sway,
In shadows of blue, forever they'll stay.

Pinecones and Pebbles Encased in Crystal

In a world of stillness, beneath the clear sky,
Pinecones lay scattered, their secrets held high.
Pebbles like jewels, so small yet profound,
Encased in the crystal where wonders abound.

A gentle embrace by the frost's icy hand,
Transforming the forest into a magical land.
Each twig and each stone tells a story or two,
Of seasons once passed and the morning dew.

Through branches adorned with a delicate sheen,
Nature displays her serene, quiet scene.
The sparkle of sunlight catches each glance,
In the heart of the wild, where dreams waltz and dance.

Amongst the pinecones, the whispers run free,
Nature's soft treasures, for all eyes to see.
With every breath taken, the magic unfolds,
In the breath of the forest, where beauty beholds.

Encased in crystal, time weaves its own thread,
Stories of life and of love truly spread.
A moment frozen in nature's embrace,
Pinecones and pebbles, a timeless grace.

Frozen Echoes of the Whispering Wind

The wind carries whispers through branches so bare,
Frozen echoes dance in the crisp morning air.
Each note tells a tale of the season's great sway,
In the quiet of winter, where shadows play.

Breath of the forest, both gentle and wild,
Paints the landscape with each flurry compiled.
A hush fills the space, as if time stands still,
Listening closely, one can feel the thrill.

The frostbitten grass catches light like a dream,
While shadows and shimmer create a soft gleam.
The wind's lullaby sings of secrets untold,
In the depths of the forest, where wonders unfold.

With every gust, a memory takes flight,
Echoes of moments lost in the night.
The heart of the wild beats soft and sincere,
In the frozen embrace, where all is clear.

In the realm of the wind, the stories align,
Frozen echoes of the past forever entwine.
Nature's symphony, in silence, it spins,
As the frozen world hums with the whispering winds.

The Sigh of an Icy Heart

In the stillness of the night,
Whispers echo, cold and bright.
A heart encased in frozen shades,
Secrets buried, love evades.

Snowflakes dance like silent tears,
Each one holding all my fears.
A fading warmth, a ghostly spark,
Lost in shadows, lost in dark.

Through the chill, a distant call,
Hope emerges, yet feels small.
Melodies from winter's song,
Echo within, where hearts belong.

Underneath the ice so deep,
Lies a promise I must keep.
A sigh escapes, the heart does yearn,
For warmth and love, a sacred fern.

With every breath, the frost will fade,
Revealing what the heart has made.
An icy heart begins to thaw,
In love's embrace, I find my awe.

Frozen Memories Beneath the Boughs

Beneath the branches, still and bare,
Lie memories lost in winter's care.
Footprints buried in the snow,
Whispers of times that used to glow.

A laughter shared, now hushed and gone,
Echoes linger as dusk moves on.
Shadows stretch where sunlight played,
In frozen frames, sweet moments laid.

The crunch of snow, a soft refrain,
A haunting song, both joy and pain.
With every gust, a story's told,
Of dreams once warm, now icy cold.

Boughs heavy with the weight of frost,
Bear witness to the love that's lost.
Yet in the silence, hope remains,
In winter's heart, new life regains.

As seasons turn, the thaw will come,
Awakening all, with love's soft hum.
Beneath the boughs, memories breathe,
In every heartbeat, we believe.

Sparkling Secrets in the Shivering Glade

In the glade where silence reigns,
Sparkling secrets kiss the panes.
Frosty charms on branches cling,
Winter's breath, a whispering.

Glittering flakes like diamonds fall,
Draped around the ancient walls.
Nature's silence speaks so loud,
Wrapped in winter's fragile shroud.

Among the trees, shadows play,
Dancing softly, night and day.
Hidden truths and dreams entwine,
In the glade, where hearts align.

A shiver runs through every leaf,
Caressing pain, embracing grief.
Yet in the chill, the warmth resides,
In sparkling secrets time abides.

When spring arrives, the thaw will sing,
Unfolding each and every thing.
From frozen depths, new life will rise,
In the glade, beneath the skies.

Lullabies of the Wintered Glens

In the glens where shadows lay,
Lullabies of winter play.
Softly sung by winds that weave,
Tales of loss and dreams that grieve.

Stars above, they gently glow,
Guiding hearts through ice and snow.
Melodies drift on the breeze,
Carrying hopes beneath the trees.

Crystals shimmer in moonlight's gaze,
Reflecting nights of mystic haze.
In every note, a story spins,
Of battles lost and quiet wins.

Whispers cradle the sleeping earth,
Holding secrets of rebirth.
In winter's grip, the glens do sigh,
Awaiting spring's sweet lullaby.

As time moves on and seasons blend,
Nature's song will never end.
For in the hearts of those who dream,
Lies lullabies like flowing streams.

Twilight Icescape

The sun dips low in the pale sky,
Chill whispers through the frozen pines,
Shadows dance on the glistening snow,
Nature's breath, a soft, silent sigh.

Icicles glint like delicate stars,
Frosted branches weave tales in white,
The world wrapped in a velvety hush,
Quietude reigns as day turns to night.

Footprints linger on the icy ground,
Each step a promise, a story shared,
In the twilight, magic can be found,
A fleeting moment, beautifully rare.

Colors fade in the dimming light,
Pastel shades of cobalt and jade,
The horizon mingles with the night,
In twilight's arms, dreams are made.

With every breath, the air crystallizes,
A wonderland, pure and serene,
In twilight's glow, joy realizes,
Nature's palette lends a vivid sheen.

Dappled Light, A Symphony of Crystals and Shadows

Sunlight filters through leafy canopies,
Creating pools of warm, golden hue,
Dancing shadows on the vibrant floor,
Nature's canvas, ever fresh and new.

The brook sings soft in a gentle flow,
Reflecting the sparkle of the day,
Every ripple tells a story bright,
A symphony woven in light's ballet.

Leaves shimmer like jewels in the breeze,
Colorful whispers, the air alive,
Each moment a brushstroke from above,
Where nature's harmony starts to thrive.

Cascading rays blend dark and light,
The symphony plays in a charming delight,
Echoes of laughter and joy abound,
In this serene, enchanted site.

As day drifts slowly into the night,
Stars awaken, ready to play,
Dappled dreams weave through the twilight,
In this melody where shadows sway.

The Melancholy of Winter's Breath

The air turns frigid, crisp and clear,
Winter's breath whispers soft and low,
Sleepy fields wait in quiet fear,
Blanketed in a shimmering snow.

Every tree stands stoic and bare,
Branches adorned like fragile lace,
In the stillness, a longing stare,
For warmth and colors, a hopeful grace.

As dusk settles with a heavy heart,
The world shrouded in dim, cold light,
Even the stars seem to play a part,
Casting shadows, retreating from sight.

Time drifts slowly as hours blend,
In this frozen realm of frozen dreams,
Each moment feels like an aching end,
Where silence echoes and stillness gleams.

Yet in this sorrow, a beauty lies,
A tranquil peace amidst the cold,
For winter's breath holds a soft disguise,
A promise of springs yet to unfold.

Fragments of Cold Beneath Ancient Roots

Beneath the frost, secrets lie deep,
Whispers of ages wrapped in the earth,
Silent guardians that vigil keep,
Tracing the lines of existence and birth.

Roots intertwine, a tangled embrace,
Holding the stories of seasons past,
Where shadows linger, time starts to race,
In the dark, the die has been cast.

The chill burrows into the dark clay,
Cradling remnants of life long gone,
In the heart of winter's stark ballet,
Ancient echoes linger, whisper on.

While the air bites with a wintry sting,
Life waits patiently, a tender pause,
For every fragment holds promise of spring,
A rebirth waiting to find its cause.

In the stillness, hope finds its way,
Beneath the cold, life stirs to renew,
As ancient roots bide time to convey,
That even in stillness, life sees it through.

Nibbled Paths on a Crystal Carpet

In the hush of early morn,
Footprints trace a fleeting path,
Where whispers dance with frosted air,
And dreams unfold in nature's bath.

Sparkling gems on every blade,
A shimmer graces all around,
Nature's art, a soft parade,
In silence, beauty can be found.

Colors merge in winter's grace,
Each step tells a hidden tale,
A journey woven in this space,
Where every breath is crystal pale.

As shadows lengthen, daylight wanes,
The paths fade into twilight's sigh,
Yet echoes linger, sweet refrains,
Of nibbled trails beneath the sky.

Resilient, the earth stands still,
Holding secrets through the night,
In the heart, a tender thrill,
For every step brings pure delight.

Frosted Memories Beneath the Aged Oak

Beneath the branches, dreams reside,
Frost clings softly, whispers low,
Time's embrace, a gentle guide,
Where memories and shadows flow.

The ancient bark, a witness true,
To stories etched through every year,
In icy stillness, life renews,
Each breath, a note of silent cheer.

In crowded nooks, the chill remains,
Crystalline laughter fills the air,
As nature plays her timeless games,
Each frame of frost, a tale laid bare.

Leaves like silver catch the sun,
Drifting softly, dreams would weave,
In harmony, the song's begun,
Beneath the oak, we still believe.

So let us gather, hand in hand,
With icy whispers shared anew,
For in this frosted, sacred land,
Our hearts will always find their view.

Winter's Breath on Sleeping Leaves

A shroud of white on slumbered ground,
Winter breathes its icy sigh,
In dreams beneath, life's stirrings found,
As shadows dance and moments fly.

Leaves lay still in frosted trance,
Awaiting warmth from sun's embrace,
In this stillness, a quiet chance,
To gather strength, to find our place.

Crystal wisps float on the breeze,
Ghostly threads of seasons past,
Bringing forth a sense of ease,
In nature, shadows will be cast.

Through every flake, stories weave,
A tapestry of silent cheer,
As stars above in night believe,
That spring will come, and dreams draw near.

For winter's breath, though cold and deep,
Holds promises that softly glow,
In every silence, secrets seep,
And life awaits beneath the snow.

Specters of Chill in the Gnarled Thicket

In twisted paths of silent night,
Specters roam the shadowed wood,
With whispers woven, pure delight,
In breath of frost, a fleeting mood.

Gnarled branches, secrets keep,
Beneath the moon, a silver glow,
In chilling silence, dreams can seep,
Where shadows dance, and yet we know.

Frosted edges, a mystical trail,
Tales of old on every leaf,
In winter's grasp, we softly hail,
Each haunting echo, sweet relief.

Through brambles thick, and darkness deep,
The chill ignites a spark within,
For in the night, our spirits leap,
As whispers guide us from the din.

Each step a pulse of frozen air,
Beneath a sky of endless dreams,
In specters' dance, we find our care,
In gnarled thicket, silent beams.

Whispers in the Winter Shade

In the silence, shadows play,
Winter whispers, soft and gray.
Trees stand tall, their branches bare,
A world of calm, a world of care.

Footsteps muffled, crunch of snow,
Every breath a cloud, a glow.
Nature sleeps, in quiet dreams,
Where light and dark weave silent themes.

The chilling breeze, a gentle sigh,
Beneath the pale and leaden sky.
Time drifts slow, a ghostly waltz,
Echoes linger, no faults to exalts.

Frosty whispers weave the night,
Under stars, a silver light.
Softly spoken, secrets spun,
Winter's tales have just begun.

In the hush, my thoughts take flight,
Carried by the silent night.
In the cold, I find my peace,
In winter's arms, my soul's release.

Silent Crystals on Twisted Branches

Beneath the weight of winter's breath,
Crystals sparkle, dance with death.
Twisted branches, strong and bold,
Guarding stories yet untold.

A tapestry of ice adorned,
Nature's beauty, widely mourned.
Each drop of frost, a fleeting breath,
In silent night, they pause from death.

Moonlight glimmers on the hue,
Soft blue tones, a world askew.
Each crystal glows with tales of yore,
A quiet heart forevermore.

Branches whisper to the ground,
In every rustle, secrets found.
Silent stories, echoes clear,
Mark the path, where dreams adhere.

In the stillness, magic brews,
A symphony of winter's muse.
Silent crystals, twisted grace,
Compose the symphony of space.

The Chill of Twilight Fables

Twilight falls like a soft embrace,
Color fades, leaves a trace.
The chill of dusk wraps around,
In whispered tales, new dreams found.

Shadows lengthen, stretching wide,
In the gloaming, secrets bide.
Footsteps echo, muted, slow,
Where twilight's magic begins to flow.

Stars ignite against the night,
Their distant glow, a fragile light.
Fables linger in the air,
Inviting all who stop and stare.

Stories spun from silver threads,
In twilight's hush, where longing spreads.
Fables pulse beneath the skin,
Awakening the dreams within.

In the chill, the heart will race,
Drawn to the twilight's gentle grace.
Every moment, woven tight,
Twilight weaves the stars in flight.

Frosted Dreams Beneath the Canopy

Underneath the frosted trees,
Dreams are captured in the breeze.
Whispers echo, soft and clear,
Beneath the branches, ever near.

Gentle snowflakes kiss the ground,
In their dance, lost thoughts are found.
A canopy of white and gray,
Where night and day blend and sway.

Every breath a shimmering sigh,
Clouding visions as we try.
To grasp the dreams, elusive, bright,
Encased in frost, they dim the night.

Moments linger, catching light,
In frosted dreams, our hearts take flight.
A world reborn in winter's hue,
Where silence speaks and whispers true.

Under canopies, we find our way,
Through the frosted paths we stray.
Embracing dreams, both vast and deep,
In nature's arms, our spirits leap.

Frost-Laden Tales of the Old Forest

Whispers of snow in ancient trees,
Carrying secrets on the chilly breeze.
Each branch a story, each trunk a song,
Echoes of ages where spirits belong.

A carpet of white, the ground does wear,
Frosted beauty, so fragile and rare.
Creatures pause, held by winter's embrace,
In this enchanted, enchanted place.

Footsteps crunch on the frozen leaves,
A moment of magic, the heart believes.
Moonlight dances on shadows cast,
A glimpse of the future, a nod to the past.

The air is thick with stories untold,
Of lovers and legends, both brave and bold.
Through lingering mist, a faint glimmer glows,
In frost-laden tales, the old forest knows.

The Blue Hues of Winter's Solitude

Under the sky where silence reigns,
A blanket of blue, where calm remains.
In frozen stillness, the world holds its breath,
In the chill of the air, a whisper of death.

Frosted branches, a delicate lace,
Painting the landscape, a tranquil space.
Footprints of time mark the soft, pale ground,
Echoes of dreams in winter abound.

The river stands still, a mirror of sky,
Reflecting the stillness where spirits fly.
A hush falls over the glittering scene,
In the heart of winter, serene yet unseen.

Shadows stretch long as the daylight fades,
In twilight's embrace, a mystery wades.
Beneath the cold stars, a soft sigh escapes,
In the blue hues of night, the heart reshapes.

Shadows Dance with the Winter Wind

In the still of the night, shadows take flight,
Dancing and whirling, a swirling delight.
The wind whispers secrets, old and bold,
As branches twist gently, their stories told.

A chorus of sighs fills the icy air,
Nature's own rhythm, wild and rare.
With every gust, a tale is spun,
Of winter's embrace, where dreams have run.

Ghostly figures flit 'neath the pale moon's glow,
Crafting an elegance in the soft, white snow.
With laughter and echoes, they twirl and sway,
Painting the night in shadows of gray.

As dawn approaches, the magic dissolves,
Yet in the chill morning, the spirit evolves.
For shadows may vanish, but memories bind,
In the heart of the night, the winter wind finds.

Crystalized Wishes on the Frosty Path

Each step is a whisper, a wish in the frost,
Where dreams crystallize, and nothing is lost.
A glimmer of hope in the morning dew,
Nature holds secrets, both old and new.

The path is a canvas, painted in white,
With wishes and wonders that twinkle in light.
Every sparkle shines bright, a promise untold,
In the crystalized moments, our hearts are bold.

Frosty breath mingles with chill in the air,
A dance of enchantment, a spell to share.
With every frost-kissed leaf, stories unfold,
As wishes take shape in the chill of the cold.

Through this winter wonder, we wander and roam,
Finding the warmth of a distant home.
In every soft footprint, a dream we leave,
With crystalized wishes, we dare to believe.

A Symphony of Icicles and Silence

In the stillness, ice refrains,
A crystal song that remains.
Beneath the weight of silent night,
Icicles reflect a pale light.

Each droplet hangs like fate's embrace,
A fleeting moment, a cold trace.
Fractured whispers, soft and clear,
Echoes of what we hold dear.

Nature's breath, a frozen hush,
In this quiet, time turns to dust.
Melodies dance on icy strings,
The heart of winter softly sings.

As shadows shift from light to shade,
Each glimmer glistens, unafraid.
A symphony born from the chill,
In every note, a world stands still.

Listen close, the beauty flows,
In this silence, the spirit grows.
Icicles sway in gentle breeze,
A tranquil moment, the soul's release.

Beneath the Whispering Pines

In the forest, secrets breathe,
Whispers carried by the leaves.
Pines participate in the song,
In their shade, we all belong.

Branches sway with gentle grace,
Nature's symphony finds its place.
Underfoot, the needles fall,
Softly cushioning our call.

Sunlight filters, dappled light,
Golden hues amidst the night.
In this refuge, hearts entwine,
Beneath the pines, the world aligns.

Time stands still, a sacred space,
Each moment holds a warm embrace.
With every breath, the spirit soars,
In the woods, the soul restores.

Whispered tales of ages past,
In each breeze, a friendship cast.
Together here, we find our way,
Beneath the pines, we choose to stay.

Timeless Beauty in Reluctant Slumber

In the hush of winter's chill,
Nature rests, a tranquil will.
Blankets made of purest white,
Cradling life in the soft night.

Dreams awaken, softly spun,
While the snowflakes fall, one by one.
In reluctant slumber, they wait,
For the sunshine to set them straight.

Timeless beauty, wrapped in peace,
In this stillness, worries cease.
Nature holds her breath with grace,
In every corner, a hidden place.

Buds beneath the blanket sigh,
While winter veils the earth nearby.
In silence, life prepares to bloom,
Underneath the icy gloom.

When warmth returns, they'll rise and stretch,
Creative forms that nature sketches.
For now, we watch the snowflakes dance,
In this slumber, there's romance.

Glacial Petals Springing from the Earth

As frost gives way to morning light,
Petals bloom in the soft twilight.
From icy graves, they break the mold,
In tender hues, their stories told.

Glacial whispers in the air,
Nature's promise, sweet and rare.
Every blossom, a tale of grace,
Springing forth from a frozen place.

Colors vibrant, chasing gloom,
Awakening the dormant bloom.
Hope emerges, resilient and fierce,
Through the ice, its heart will pierce.

Petals cradle the morning dew,
In their dance, the earth renews.
With each breath, life finds its way,
In the warmth of a dawning day.

Emerging beauty, a triumph grand,
Against the chill, we take a stand.
Glacial petals, in their mirth,
Springing forth, they bless the earth.

Starlit Crystals and Woodland Murmurs

In the night, the crystals gleam,
Beneath the stars, a gentle dream.
Whispers float through leaves so green,
Woodland secrets, softly seen.

Moonlit paths, where shadows sway,
Softly guiding, lost hearts stay.
Nature's breath in cool embrace,
Every rustle, a hidden grace.

Crickets sing their evening song,
In the dark, where night feels long.
Owls call out, wise and deep,
Guardians of the woods, they keep.

Stars like diamonds, scattered wide,
In this realm, we dare to bide.
Time stands still, the world fades away,
In starlit crystals, we long to stay.

With each murmur from the trees,
Echoes dance upon the breeze.
Comfort found in nature's hush,
In the night, we find our rush.

The Whispering Frost and the Ancient Trees

Frost-kissed branches, glistening white,
Guardians of the silent night.
Tales of old in whispers flow,
In the stillness, secrets grow.

Ancient trees with stories held,
In their bark, life's dreams repelled.
Frosty breath wraps every bough,
Nature's art, a solemn vow.

Underneath the moon's soft gaze,
Truths emerge in twilight's haze.
Frost paints magic on each leaf,
In the quiet, find relief.

Rustling winds, a gentle sigh,
As the stars begin to fly.
Every whisper, a soft tune,
Embraced beneath the silver moon.

The ancient woods hold time's embrace,
In the frost, we find our place.
Nature speaks in quiet charms,
Wrapped in frost, we feel its arms.

Shards of Ice in the Dim Light

Shards of ice catch the glow,
Light refracts, a dancing show.
In the shadows, silence dwells,
Secrets held, no one tells.

Glistening edges, sharp and clear,
Echoes of the past, so near.
Frigid breath of winter's hand,
Frozen beauty, quiet stand.

Dim light flickers on the ground,
In this realm, peace can be found.
Chill that stirs the heart to think,
Nature's art in every blink.

Among the shards, silence reigns,
In the cold, there's no more pain.
Frozen pieces, memories bright,
Whispers hidden in the night.

When the morning casts its rays,
Ice will melt in gentle plays.
Yet in dim light, truth remains,
Shards of ice in nature's chains.

Twilight's Touch on Sinister Branches

Twilight descends with phantom light,
Casting shadows, deep as night.
Sinister branches stretch and creep,
In their grasp, old secrets sleep.

Whispers flow through tangled wood,
Echoes of things misunderstood.
Every rustle hides a tale,
In the dark, sharp winds prevail.

Moonbeams pierce the darkened sky,
As unseen creatures softly cry.
Within the gloom, a world resides,
Where twilight's magic gently glides.

Branches twist with eerie grace,
Shadowed forms begin to trace.
In the fading, light grows low,
Secrets dark begin to show.

Yet in the stillness, beauty lies,
Twilight's touch, a soft disguise.
Sinister branches, yet so bright,
Hold the mysteries of the night.

Echoes of Silence and Shimmering Deceit

In shadows deep, whispers dwell,
A tale of trust, a fragile shell.
Reflections dance in fleeting light,
Deceit's embrace, a cold goodnight.

The echoes fade, yet linger still,
A haunting tune, a bitter thrill.
Promises shatter like broken glass,
In silence sweet, the moments pass.

Beneath the surface, truth will hide,
Only to rise, as waves collide.
The heart will ache, the soul will weep,
In shadows deep, where secrets creep.

With every sigh, a story spun,
A web of dreams, a race not run.
In silence loud, the echoes call,
A fractured world where shadows fall.

So tread with care, in twilight's glow,
For shimmering lies may steal the show.
Beneath the veneer, the scars run deep,
In echoes of silence, secrets keep.

In the Heart of the Winter Clearing

Beneath the frost, the earth lies still,
A whispered breath, a quiet thrill.
The pines stand tall, adorned in white,
In winter's arms, a frosty night.

A clearing vast, where shadows play,
With every flake, the world turns gray.
The air so crisp, it bites the skin,
Yet beauty thrives where dreams begin.

In distant woods, a silence reigns,
Amongst the trees, the stillness gains.
A glimmer shines, a spark of hope,
In every heart, we learn to cope.

The moon ascends, a silver queen,
Casting shadows where life once gleaned.
In the heart of night, a glow appears,
Warming the chill, dispelling fears.

So pause awhile, embrace the peace,
In winter's grasp, let troubles cease.
For in the clearing, life unveils,
A promise held, where time prevails.

The Lament of the Ice-Bound Trees

In silence cold, the trees do weep,
Their branches bare, in winter's keep.
Each crystal tear, a tale of woe,
The ice-bound limbs, a heart laid low.

With every gust, they sway and bend,
A mournful song, a broken friend.
The winter winds, a cruel embrace,
In their stillness, a hollow space.

Yet deep within, a pulse remains,
A whisper soft, amidst the pains.
The roots are strong, though scars may show,
In icy grip, the life must flow.

When spring arrives, the thaw will come,
To break the chains, to banish numb.
And though they sigh in haunting tunes,
The ice-bound trees will greet the moons.

For every winter, spring ignites,
With vibrant blooms and warmer nights.
Hope lingers still, beneath the frost,
In every loss, there's something tossed.

Shimmering Silence Beneath the Moonlight

In twilight's veil, the world stands still,
A whispered hush, a tranquil thrill.
The moonlight spills on tranquil seas,
Embracing night with gentle pleas.

Stars twinkle soft in velvet skies,
As silence blankets, whispers rise.
The shimmering glow, a soothing balm,
In night's embrace, a binding calm.

Each ripple sings a quiet tune,
Reflecting dreams beneath the moon.
The world is hushed, as hearts comply,
In shimmering silence, no need to try.

With every breath, the night unfolds,
A tapestry of stories told.
In tranquil depths, where shadows play,
The night reveals what words can't say.

So linger long, in moonlight's grace,
Allow the silence, time to chase.
For in that stillness, truth will find,
A shimmering peace, a solace kind.

Midnight Stroll through a Crystal Forest

Beneath the stars, the trees stand tall,
Their branches shimmer, a glistening sprawl.
The moonlight dances on the frozen ground,
In this quiet magic, peace is found.

Whispers of snowflakes softly fall,
As gentle breezes echo their call.
Footsteps crunch through the icy night,
A heart awakens to pure delight.

Each crystal twig, a story to share,
In nature's silence, we breathe the air.
With every glance, the beauty grows,
In this enchanted world, my spirit flows.

Glistening paths lead deeper still,
A sense of wonder, an endless thrill.
The forest wraps me in its embrace,
Midnight whispers, a sacred place.

As dawn approaches, a hint of light,
The forest fades softly into the night.
Yet in my heart, its magic will stay,
In dreams of crystal, I'm never far away.

Frosted Pines against a Dusk Sky

Tall pines outline a dusky hue,
Softly twinkling in evening's brew.
Gold and purple, a canvas so wide,
Nature's palette at evening's side.

Breathless wonder as the night draws near,
A chill in the air, but the heart feels clear.
Frosted needles catch the fading light,
In this serene moment, all feels right.

Birdsong quiets as shadows creep,
Wrapped in calm, the world seems to sleep.
With each moment, the dusk grows bold,
In the embrace of twilight, stories unfold.

Stars twinkle high, a shimmering cloak,
The whisper of night, a gentle stroke.
Pines stand proud beneath the vast sky,
In their stillness, I too want to fly.

As darkness blankets the rolling hills,
The beauty lingers, a heart that fills.
In this frost-kissed realm, dreams are spun,
The dusk and the pines, forever as one.

Entranced by the Stillness of the Frost

In the hush of dawn, frost paints the ground,
A world transformed, magic is found.
Each crystal breath, a whisper so sweet,
In stillness, the world feels utterly complete.

The branches heavy, draped in white,
Glisten softly in morning light.
A silent beauty, a gentle pause,
Inviting reflection, and soft applause.

Footprints left, a journey begun,
Through frosted fields, under the sun.
Each step a dance, a moment so rare,
Entranced by the stillness, life seems to share.

As time unfolds in shimmering lace,
Nature's masterpiece, a wondrous space.
Golden sunbeams peek through the frost,
In this stillness, we ponder what's lost.

With every breath, winter sings low,
A chorus of peace in the cold wind's flow.
Entranced by the beauty that nature provides,
In silence I walk, where my spirit abides.

A Shimmering Path of Icy Delights

Glimmers of silver on the frozen trail,
Each step I take tells a wondrous tale.
Icy delights sparkle bright and clear,
Guiding me onward, drawing me near.

With the touch of frost beneath my feet,
Nature's treasures, a magical feat.
Windows of crystal frame the scene,
Each corner turned reveals something serene.

Quiet enchantment fills the air,
The world feels light, devoid of care.
A shimmering path, a secret untold,
In each icy glimmer, I find pure gold.

Frost clings softly to every leaf,
A moment of stillness, beyond belief.
I pause to wonder at beauty so rare,
In this shimmering world, I breathe the air.

Through the icy woods, my heart takes flight,
Embracing the magic of the night.
Laughter of snowflakes, a delicate dance,
On this shimmering path, I find my chance.

Ghostly Figures in the Icy Mist

In the depths of the night, shadows glide,
Whispers of secrets, where dreams confide.
Frozen reflections dance on the ground,
Silent echoes of memories found.

Veils of white shroud the trees' tall embrace,
Hushed tales linger in this ethereal space.
Figures appear, just out of reach,
Fleeting reminders of lessons they teach.

Ghostly forms in a world so still,
Carried by winds, as they bend to will.
Drifting through time, they wander and roam,
Searching for solace, a path to their home.

Beneath the pale moon, they silently glide,
In the heart of the mist, their spirits reside.
A dance of the lost, in the chill of the night,
Ghostly figures fading, out of our sight.

Every heartbeat echoes, a soft, distant call,
In the icy mist, where shadows enthrall.
They weave through the silence, a haunting refrain,
In the world of the lost, forever remain.

The Stillness of the Snow-Blanketed World

A hushed peace settles, soft flakes descend,
Covering earth like a welcoming friend.
Each step is muffled, a gentle embrace,
In the stillness of winter, time finds its pace.

Trees stand adorned in crystalline white,
Branches bowed low, a serene, soft sight.
Quietly whispering, the winds seem to sing,
Songs of the frosty, enchanting spring.

Footprints left behind, where journeys once tread,
Memories linger, stories unsaid.
The snow coats the world in a blanket so pure,
A soft, peaceful slumber, the heart does secure.

Stars twinkle brightly in the velvet sky,
Lighting the night as the moon whispers by.
In this ethereal world, dreams come to play,
Beneath the still snowfall, worries drift away.

The air crisp and clear, like a sweet lullaby,
Breath visible, rising like hope to the sky.
In the stillness of winter, all feels just right,
Wrapped in the warmth of the soft, snowy night.

Frost's Gentle Caress on Every Leaf

Morning unveils a magical sight,
Frost kisses leaves with soft, shimmering light.
Nature adorned in a delicate lace,
Each breath of the dawn, a tranquil embrace.

The whispers of winter dance through the trees,
Awakening beauty, carried by the breeze.
Every twig sparkles, a diamond display,
Nature's own artwork, too lovely to fray.

As sunlight breaks forth, the frost starts to fade,
Revealing the colors, in shadows they played.
Each leaf a canvas, each branch a song,
In the serenade of nature, we all belong.

Moments of magic held close to the heart,
In the chill of the morning, where wonders depart.
Frost's gentle caress, a soft lull of peace,
In the still of the dawn, all troubles find cease.

A world dressed in silver, a timeless embrace,
Frost brings a hush to this sacred space.
In nature's sweet realm, tranquility thrives,
As frost marks the moments, where beauty survives.

Midnight Frost and Forgotten Trails

Under the cloak of a moonlit night,
Midnight frost glistens, a mesmerizing sight.
Forgotten trails linger, lost in the dark,
Whispers of journeys, a fading spark.

Cold air wraps round like a tender shawl,
Tales intertwined in the silence of all.
Each breath a plume, drifting under the stars,
Mapping the stories written in scars.

The crunch of the frost beneath weary feet,
Echoes of wanderers' hearts in retreat.
Paths once vibrant now shrouded in chill,
Time bears its witness, yet echoes still thrill.

A canvas of white where dreams softly tread,
Midnight's embrace whispers hopes long since fled.
In the arms of the night, where memories rest,
The spirit of wanderers feels ever blessed.

Each star a promise, a guide from above,
Lighting the trails that we wander in love.
As midnight frost blankets the earth's gentle trails,
We walk in silence, where the heart never fails.

The Glassy Veil of an Icy Dawn

A world adorned in crystal light,
The sun peeks through a frosty night.
Each breath a whisper, crisp and clear,
Nature stirs as dawn draws near.

Trees stand tall, their branches lace,
Frozen jewels in a dainty grace.
The air is sharp, the silence deep,
Awakening dreams from winter's sleep.

Footprints crunch on powdery ground,
In this tranquil spell, peace is found.
The glassy veil enfolds the sky,
As morning glories softly sigh.

Birds will chirp as daylight grows,
To banish shadows, cast off woes.
The icy dawn unveils its charm,
In nature's embrace, we find our calm.

Spirits of Winter in the Mystic Grove

In the grove where shadows creep,
Whispering winds begin to weep.
Spirits dance in frosted air,
Awakening the night's old flare.

Moonlight bathes the silent trees,
Carried through on chilly breeze.
Mystic echoes call the brave,
To wander paths the ancients paved.

Footfalls light on ancient earth,
In the stillness, find rebirth.
Spirits linger, soft and shy,
Guiding souls where secrets lie.

Frosted whispers fill the night,
With tales of love, of loss, of light.
In this grove of dreams and sighs,
Winter's magic never dies.

Murmurs of the Frosted Foliage

Beneath the boughs of winter's breath,
  Silent secrets hide, life and death.
  Frosted leaves in shimmered hush,
    Murmur softly; wild hearts rush.

  Each flake a note, a gentle song,
  Nature's chorus, sweet and strong.
    Unseen voices linger near,
    In frosted foliage, they appear.

The world is wrapped in soft embrace,
A white-washed canvas, tranquil space.
  Tread lightly on this fragile ground,
  In whispers lost, connections found.

    Winds will carry tales of old,
  Of dreams remembered, stories told.
    In murmurs soft as falling snow,
  The heart knows where it longs to go.

Dreams Wrapped in Snowflakes' Touch

In dreams wrapped soft like fallen flakes,
Each wish a path the heart now takes.
Whispers drift on twilight's tide,
With every snowfall, worlds collide.

A tapestry of white unfolds,
In every flake, a truth retold.
The sky kisses the silent ground,
In winter's arms, love can be found.

Children laugh, let spirit soar,
As snowflakes swirl from heaven's door.
They dance around in frosty bliss,
In fleeting moments, life's sweet kiss.

The night is cloaked in gentle dreams,
Where silver moonlight softly gleams.
With every breath, our hopes ignite,
In snowflakes' touch, we find the light.

The Hushed Song of the Icebound Trail

Whispers of frost in the still night air,
Footsteps muffled, wrapped in the chill.
A crystalline path leads away from despair,
Shadows dance softly, a fleeting thrill.

Moonlight drapes silver on branches so bare,
Glimmers of magic in every breath taken.
The world is enchanted, held in its snare,
A symphony formed, yet never awakened.

Each step a note in the serene ballad,
Nature's own echo, a lullaby's grace.
Silence prevails, on memory's salad,
In nature's embrace, all worries erase.

Icebergs shimmer in the distance so bright,
Glistening prisms of blue and of white.
The path stretches onward, a shimmering sight,
In the hush of the night, all feels just right.

With wonder we wander, hearts open wide,
Finding our peace where the wild things dwell.
In the song of the ice, through the dusk we glide,
Carving our stories in time's frozen shell.

Caresses of Cold in the Waking Woods

Morning breaks softly, wrapped in the frost,
Branches breathe whispers of winter's embrace.
Nature awakens, no moment is lost,
Fingers of cold travel over each space.

Pine trees stand tall under blankets of white,
Each flake a treasure, a delicate dance.
Nature's artwork shines, pure and so bright,
The woods come alive in nature's romance.

A hush fills the air with the softest sigh,
And laughter of streams breaks the silence tight.
Crystals of dew form a glimmering sky,
As sunbeams spill golden, sharing the light.

Footsteps echo through these resplendent halls,
Each step artfully falls on carpeted gold.
Echoes of laughter through silent white walls,
In these caresses, our secrets unfold.

This world holds a magic, so tender and bold,
Wrapped in the chill of the waking woods' grace.
In caresses of cold, our spirits consoled,
Harmonies linger, in nature's embrace.

When Silence Meets Chilled Twilight

Twilight descends, painting shadows with frost,
   Gentle the whisper of dusk in the sky.
  As daylight succumbs, no moment is lost,
The world holds its breath, and dreams come to lie.

   Silence cascades on the edge of the night,
   Crickets are stitching their tunes in the air.
   Stars begin twinkling, a delicate sight,
  Winking their secrets, a lover's soft stare.

The trees stand as sentinels, regal and still,
  Guardians of whispers, their stories untold.
The warmth of the twilight, a promise to fill,
Each heartbeat a rhythm, in silence controlled.

  Moonrise embraces the hushed, starry veil,
   Casting its glow on the world far below.
In stillness, the heart knows the tales that prevail,
When silence meets twilight, and magic will flow.

  As dreams intertwine in the cool evening haze,
   Fates intertwining, like shadows they weave.
  A promise to cherish in the briefest of days,
When silence meets twilight, we dare to believe.

Enchantment in the Cobalt Hues

Deep in the night, where the shadows collide,
Cobalt horizons stretch far and away.
The stars weave their magic, the secrets they hide,
In whispers of dreams as the night turns to day.

Each twinkle a story, each shimmer a sigh,
Painting the canvas of dusk with delight.
The moon's gentle presence, a watchful eye,
Guides us through depths of the velvety night.

The air is electric, a pulse in our veins,
With enchantment lurking in corners unseen.
Through cobalt blue heavens, our spirit regains,
A beauty, a wonder, a soft, soothing sheen.

A dance in the shadows, two hearts intertwine,
Lost in the magic of soft midnight views.
With every heartbeat, the universe signs,
A pact of forever, in cobalt hues.

As dawn starts to whisper and bid us goodbye,
Colors emerge from the calm velvet sea.
In enchantment we stand, with love in our eye,
Cobalt reflections, forever set free.

Rime-Encased Dreams in the Woodland Realm

In the quiet woods where shadows play,
Rime encases dreams in delicate sway.
Whispers of frost in the fading light,
Sprinkling magic through the velvet night.

Branches adorned with crystalline lace,
Hiding secrets in their icy embrace.
Moonbeams dance on the tranquil ground,
Where frozen wonders can gently be found.

Soft is the sigh of the wandering breeze,
Carrying dreams beneath ancient trees.
Echoes of laughter lost in the chill,
Wrap around hearts with a shimmering thrill.

Time gently pauses in this serene place,
Where rime-encased visions find their grace.
Through the still air, a melody hums,
Guiding the lost where the white silence comes.

Here in the twilight, all worries cease,
Wrapped in the tapestry of winter's peace.
The soul finds solace, a moment's reprieve,
In the woodland realm where we dare to believe.

Frozen Echoes of the Lost Traveler

On winding paths through the snow-clad trees,
Echoes of footsteps dance with the breeze.
A traveler lost in the cold, dark night,
Seeking a beacon, a flicker of light.

The moon hangs low, a lantern so pale,
Guiding the heart that has begun to fail.
Whispers of frost haunt the silent way,
In frozen echoes where shadows betray.

Memories linger in the biting air,
Fleeting moments that vanished with care.
Time distorts in this icy domain,
As dreams melt away like the falling rain.

Across the expanse of this shimmering white,
Awaits a warmth hidden from sight.
A flicker, a flame, may soon break the dark,
Rekindling hope with a delicate spark.

Yet through the night, the journey persists,
With frozen echoes of shadows and mists.
And perhaps in the dawn that waits on the crest,
The lost traveler finds their heart's quiet rest.

A Tapestry of Ice and Shadows

In the realm where shadows weave and twist,
A tapestry forms in the morning mist.
Glistening threads of ice softly gleam,
Binding the essence of every dream.

Patterns emerge in the frostbitten air,
Stories of fortune and whispers of despair.
Colors of winter paint all around,
Nature's artistry in silence is found.

As sunlight breaks, the crystals ignite,
Casting reflections that dance with delight.
Each shimmering thread, a tale to be told,
Of ancient spirits and voices of old.

The world is a canvas of darkness and light,
Where ice and shadows play through the night.
With each fleeting moment, we stand in awe,
At the beauty of life as we breathe and draw.

Beneath the surface, a warmth lies in wait,
Waiting to blossom, to open the gate.
In this tapestry woven from dreams, we find,
The essence of love that transcends through time.

The Last Ember of the Woodland Glow

As twilight falls and stars take flight,
The last ember fades from the heart of night.
Among the pines where shadows creep,
A flicker of warmth in the stillness deep.

Memories dance in the soft, cool air,
Remnants of laughter and whispers of care.
The woodland glows with a gentle sigh,
As night blankets the world and the fireflies fly.

A flicker, a glow, of what once was bright,
Guiding the dreamers into the night.
In silence, the embers begin to fade,
Carrying dreams that the woodland made.

Yet in the darkness, hope finds its breath,
For even in shadows, there's light after death.
The last ember sings a lullaby sweet,
As wanderers gather where past and future meet.

In the heart of the woods, where the echoes flow,
The spirit of warmth in the chill starts to grow.
And though the night holds its secrets below,
The last ember whispers of love's gentle glow.

The Solstice Silence of Starlit Earth

Underneath the midnight sky,
Stars whisper secrets to the night,
Frozen whispers float on high,
The earth bathed in silver light.

In shadows deep, the silence grows,
Trees stand guard, their branches bare,
Moonlight dances, gentle flows,
Starlit whispers fill the air.

As winter's breath begins to sigh,
Nature waits, wrapped in peace,
Time stands still, a silent cry,
From chaos, sweet calm finds release.

In quiet moments, hearts may blend,
With twilight dreams that softly weave,
In the beauty where night shall end,
We find solace, we believe.

Beneath this vast, enchanting dome,
A tapestry of calm unfurls,
Lost wanderers find their way home,
In the starlit hush of worlds.

A Supernal Stillness in Arboreal Depths

Amidst the ancient trees so grand,
Stillness cloaks the verdant ground,
Leaves whisper secrets, hand in hand,
Their tales of time in silence found.

Sunbeams trickle, soft and gold,
Dancing through branches, warm embrace,
In this realm where wonders unfold,
Life breathes slow, finds its own pace.

Echoes of birds in twilight air,
Creation sings in muted tones,
Nature's magic lingers there,
In the heart, we feel its zone.

Shadows glide on mossy floors,
A sanctuary carved with care,
Whispers resonate from the cores,
Of life that blossoms everywhere.

In this stillness, souls awake,
Feeling roots that intertwine,
In arboreal depths we take,
The breath of nature, pure and divine.

Time's Lament in the Frozen Glade

In the frozen glade, time stands still,
Icicles hanging like silent tears,
Winter's breath speaks of lost will,
Memories fade through the bitter years.

Each snowflake falls, a whispered song,
Tracing paths of journeys past,
In the chill where we belong,
Fleeting moments, too soon cast.

Branches heavy with crystal frost,
Nature's blanket, serene and vast,
In this stillness, all seems lost,
Yet within lies a beauty unsurpassed.

Time laments in frozen air,
Echoes of laughter lost in snow,
But in the stillness, hearts repair,
As seeds of spring begin to grow.

In the glade, resilience stands,
While winter weaves its icy art,
In time's embrace, we make our plans,
For every end is a new start.

Blossom of the Frosted Spirit

In the quiet of the waking morn,
Frosted petals softly gleam,
Nature whispers to the dawn,
A tranquil ode, a waking dream.

Amidst the stillness, life finds way,
Colors break through crisp white shores,
In the chill, warmth begins to play,
As the spirit of spring restores.

Each blossom holds a tale untold,
Of life that braves the cold embrace,
In fragile beauty, bold and bold,
A spark of hope in time's swift race.

The frost may linger, but can't chain,
The yearning hearts for vibrant cheer,
As life emerges, breaking pain,
Symbol of strength with roots so dear.

In every flower, a glimpse we see,
Of tenacity in the chill,
The frosted spirit, wild and free,
Blooms forever, bending will.

Veils of Ice Through the Timeless Pines

Veils of ice drape the ancient trees,
Silent whispers ride the winter breeze.
Underneath the moon's soft, silver glow,
Shadows dance where the frostflowers grow.

Branches heavy with crystalline lace,
Nature's stillness, a hallowed embrace.
Each breath of cold a story untold,
Wrapped in the beauty, the night so bold.

Footsteps crunch on the powdered ground,
Echoes of magic in silence found.
Stars twinkle through the arching boughs,
In this moment, eternity vows.

A symphony played by the forest's breath,
Life and stillness in the hands of death.
Ethereal lights around me gleam,
In the heart of the winter's dream.

As dawn breaks gentle on the frozen scene,
Colors emerge where the night has been.
Veils of ice begin to slide away,
Revealing life in the light of day.

The Poetry of Frozen Fields

Blankets of white on the grassy ground,
Whispers of snowflakes without a sound.
Each flake a verse, unique in its fall,
Writing the tales of the wind's gentle call.

Underneath frost, the earth quietly sleeps,
Holding the secrets that winter keeps.
A canvas still, a breath held in time,
Nature composes her quiet rhyme.

Starlit nights bring a hushed serenade,
While shadows stretch in the moonlit glade.
Footsteps lead to a world of dreams,
Where cold captures warmth in silver beams.

The brook wears ice like a delicate crown,
Glistening gems as the sun dips down.
Frozen fields hum a melodious tune,
Echoing softly beneath the pale moon.

In this gallery of frost-kissed delight,
Nature's verses speak through the night.
With every breath, the enchantment grows,
In the poetry of frozen fields, love flows.

Ethereal Glades in the Depths of Winter

In ethereal glades where shadows play,
Winter's breath keeps the light at bay.
Pine-scented whispers among the trees,
Dancing with frost on a gentle breeze.

Twilight drapes the land in shades of blue,
With each quiet step, the silence grew.
Snow-laden branches bow down with grace,
Time finds its rhythm in this sacred place.

A flicker of light from a distant star,
Guides the wanderers, both near and far.
Beneath the moon's glow, the world feels true,
In these glades, dreams are born anew.

Crystal droplets fall where the rivers run,
Each a reflection of the waning sun.
Ethereal visions in the stillness blend,
Whispering softly, winter's sweet rend.

As dawn breaks gently, a canvas awakens,
The glades sing songs, no heart is forsaken.
Nature rejoices in hues of gold,
In ethereal glades, the beauty unfolds.

Glacial Dreams on the Woodland Floor

On the woodland floor where dreams take flight,
Glacial whispers weave through the night.
Snowflakes twirl in a dazzling dance,
Each one a wish, a fleeting chance.

Amidst the trees, a stillness reigns,
Frosted branches wear nature's chains.
The earth beneath a blanket so white,
Holds the secrets of long winter nights.

In the hush of the woods, all is calm,
Winter's embrace is tender and warm.
Life pauses, breath held in between,
Lost in the magic, a delicate sheen.

As the stars blink softly into the dawn,
Glacial dreams fade, but hope lingers on.
Nature's theater, forever in play,
Every step forward leads us away.

From the ice and the frost, stories emerge,
Of memories past, and futures that surge.
In the heart of the woods, we find our core,
In glacial dreams, we seek to restore.